DRAW ME AFTER

2/2016

DRAW ME

AFTER

Farrar, Straus and Giroux / New York

PETER COLE

Farrar, Straus and Giroux
120 Broadway, New York 10271

Copyright © 2022 by Peter Cole
All rights reserved
Printed in the United States of America
First edition, 2022

Deep thanks are due to friends who've lent a critical hand along the way and to
the editors of the following publications, where earlier versions of some of these
poems previously appeared: *Ayin, Caesura, Conjunctions, Harper's Magazine, Literary
Imagination, Literary Matters, The New Criterion, The Paris Review, Plume, Poetry, Rar-
itan, Salt, Subtropics, Tokyo Journal, The Yale Review, Cahiers Series* (Sylph Editions),
Terry Winters: Facts and Fictions, The Drawing Center (catalogue), *Grenfell Press, The
Lévy Gorvy Gallery Anthology, Richard Sieburth Festschrift,* and *Sensitive Reading* (in
honor of David Shulman). "Edensong," "How Could It Happen," and "As:" were
written for an oratorio (*Edensongs*), composed by Aaron Jay Kernis.

Poems by Leah Goldberg: Courtesy of HaKibbutz HaMeuchad
Poems by Yehuda Amichai: By permission of Hana Amichai
Poem by Natan Zach: By permission of the author

Images copyright © 2019 by Terry Winters,
courtesy of Matthew Marks Gallery.

Library of Congress Cataloging-in-Publication Data
Names: Cole, Peter, 1957– author.
Title: Draw me after : poems / Peter Cole.
Description: First edition. | New York : Farrar, Straus and Giroux, 2022.
Identifiers: LCCN 2022023647 | ISBN 9780374605360 (hardcover)
Subjects: LCGFT: Poetry.
Classification: LCC PS3553.O47325 D73 2022 | DDC 811/.54—
    dc23/eng/20220518
LC record available at https://lccn.loc.gov/2022023647

Our books may be purchased in bulk for promotional, educational, or business
use. Please contact your local bookseller or the Macmillan Corporate and Pre-
mium Sales Department at 1-800-221-7945, extension 5442, or by email at
MacmillanSpecialMarkets@macmillan.com.

www.fsgbooks.com
www.twitter.com/fsgbooks
www.facebook.com/fsgbooks

10 9 8 7 6 5 4 3 2 1

Each letter called, saying,
"Draw me after you, let us run."

—Zohar Chadash, Song of Songs 66c

CONTENTS

EDENSONG

Wanting song
   in the beginning
beginning to end

   now we are falling

through what's to come
   needing Eden
now we are drifting

   Eden undone

as if   from the ends
   of earth hearing
Eden's calling

   to tend and attend

now we are sprawling
   through what we've done
through what we're losing

   as what we've won

as we are falling
    as Eden is calling
earth and heaven

    wanting song

THIS PIG I

This pig I live with really
does hover over much of
what I do and say it's in
the room I lie in daily when
I try to tell myself the truth
about deceit or what I read
or just my being a jerk and lazy
pissy it brings to mind the swine
within and out of sight it's like
a shadow in its knowing how
dark at heart I am in part
it loves the muck I'm often in
the sty and stink of *me* and *my*
it's like a household deity now
whose name is mine to give and take
back in vain it's black and beautifully
sketched by Baskin in fact as though
he'd thought it a holy beast of sorts
a sacred cow or Zen bull
someone was having trouble herding
its hooves delicate as a devil's
prance cloven above the heaven
and hell of my head its law written
in red biblical letters says
for me it seems specifically—
Pig, poet, thou shalt not eat.

ALEPH : א

is all
that
might
yet
be
opening
once
again
although
a gain
is hardly
what
it brings
on,
more
a wanting
within
one,

a gap,
for song
perhaps
to start with . . .

LOOK AGAIN

for Agnes Martin

Is it stone
no it's sky
and now it's sand
or standing water
rippled under
stippled clouds
is that flowing
water framed

every possible
music there
between those lines
between these lines
drawn in grays
against the gray
to graze the light
that's there in beige's

faint blaze
ocher looming
near a crushed

eggshell blue
come into sharper
focus and viewed
in the distance
deep within

a field of wheat
or grain blown back
against the wind
or berms of germs
as grasses bloom
beyond our looking
splitting awns
of moments making

the darkness felt
as velvet black
opening into
soft distraction
a baby's breath
of news arrived
as what is near
is what was far

and could it be
her gods' excel
file   these

cells of pale
pinks a zone of
anyone's truancy
purely   sure
and all alone

in the empty
world as grid
the girded mind's
giving way to
or away
the girl within
a self that's less
and more at once

and for it all
such a patience
the slow sketch
it's a calling
being called
like a coda
code or mood
small cubes

extended reach
with smudges in each
a spot of time

or maybe not
so much a smudge
as just a clear
account of the blur
which isn't fuzzy

in its off-
center doings
slate against
that graphite scale
as quiet's score
is auburn over
scumbled gold
and ivory lurking

it's an origin
it's an end
it's an island
it's a friend
and friendship's nimbus
in the wavering
margin waves
traveling light

through rites like birth
as though it were saying

for all it's worth
look again
and again look
that's the luck
we lock ourselves
out of   look

BET : ב

Here's a bet
    on palpability—
back to what's
    beyond us and faces
a sounding that's always
    about to be
within the major
    and minor making
of letters building
    through receiving
the world anew,
    starting as two
whose secret is
    in the blessing
of beginning
    in relation
as home to wisdom's
    nameless king
or queen who isn't
    exactly seen
in the Splendor:
    O taste, it says
deep in the psalm
    we hold in our palms
(and now on our phones)—
    taste and see . . .

GOLD LINGERS

                      over the lime
small full-moon maple where
nothing I can prove appeared
like an incantation when
was it only a few years back
and then of course it slipped away
or maybe just receded some
and surfaced slightly reconfigured
in this coronal summer yard it
fills the mind beside a purple
ghost's shadows moving against
reddish stone on a wind which
kills me in the way those leaves
themselves more or less do
level something somehow blocking
a path toward that moment I'm
always about to be inside
a word of one god (it seems)
forsaken world or another
glowing with its specks of sky's
blue deflection true we
never can completely leave
behind what it is we've been through
or can we   now   what on earth
(as in heaven) are we up to?

GIMMEL : ג

Gimmel is third and like
a camel sticks its neck
out for a thing (as though

on a limb), bearing a burden.
Gimmel's a goodness actually
doing something and going

ahead with not quite
knowing what you're doing,
auguring, well, into

doing what you know
needs to be done, if not
what it's worth—which is

in part what it's worth. *Gimmel*
is one possible window
onto getting some of that

done, although in fact
it's really more like two
things combined become

a third   as a synthesis
of tensions stoked—and that's
the genius and redress

like mist in the dissonant blessing
of how it is that ruth's
in truth along with hurt.

WHAT THE BEARD SAID

Smallness of mind, the xenophobic
mystic muttered, his beard a cloud,
a little too proud, I thought, hearing:
Smallness of mind—it's what makes us
miss the greatness

                of straits opening
onto a faintness (call it largesse)
of first things' traces linking long
trails of being,

              tales of longing,
marrow in the narrow bone
of our rendered listening . . .
low—today, for instance—skies
the winter tint of tarnished vintage
silver in a kitchen drawer.
Drawing's goyish,

              said the cloud—
though you love it, over paths
you're always walking, wherever you are
(when you're able) spokes poking
out from the crown of cones or corners
you've never seen but seem to turn
within, within you.

             Time and again.
Misanthropy's end, the cloud sputtered.
Smallness of mind. Magnitude's friend.

DALET : ד

Dalet's a doorway
in Hebrew terms
derived from Phoenician
winding through time

up to De Kooning's
Door to the River—
those Ds of our own
like rounded boards

of half a table
bound to an I,
like a beggar
always at it,

always poor,
always lacking
and meaning four,
as in the directions

without and within,
but also a debt
or just the benefit
of a doubt—

a dot dented
in thinking's beginning
creation as
what-we-say-of-it

now and again
dalet's a doorway.

LATE FRAGMENTS

I.

In all we do there's at least an eighth
of a part of death. It isn't heavy.
What easy, secret grace we bear it with,
wherever we go. Through beautiful waking,
and walks, in lovers' talk, and into
distraction, forgotten deep in our being—
it's with us always. And isn't heavy.

II.

The young poet grows silent suddenly
afraid that he might speak the truth.

The old poet goes still, fearing
the finest poem
is the most feigning.

III.

And the poem I didn't write
when I wrote poems—
I remember it all,
every sound and turn of phrase.
And it won't be written still.

If I'd written it then,
its truth would have been too bare.
And were I to write it now,
it would be pure fiction.

Come . . . come to me, Muse,
and lean your whitening
head against mine.

We'll play with words—

how clear the world is
in this new game—

no now, no then
no truth, no fiction

the two pans of the scale
rising and falling—

a rhythm.

Leah Goldberg, Hebrew, 20th c.

HEY : ה

Hey you, she whispered

                    into the morning,
the he inside her bare in its longing, there
in the air of a soft address, flickering chicory-
black, like a con game—
    as the whisper drifted down
the halls of their secret echoing names . . .

SO THE DAYS

So the grayish
gauzy days
lower and lift
across this slit
like a shift
the sky wore
out its welcome
matte and weather
or not it matters
more and more
within me masked
everything fraying
at what seems
to be or will it
really is
ringing us in
its silvery lingering
white through dark
over the park
or parking lots
of time and blood
on our hands
once again

the eyes have it
listen yes
that gray in-
betweenness of this
gauze and gorgeously
bandaged day.

VAV : ו

for Geoffrey Hartman / *in memoriam*

This upright letter
bows its head
ever so slightly
out of humility
(much like Geoffrey)
toward the page

it's fixed itself
to as though
by a hook
or being hooked
really a summoning
from within

it or him
to listen hard
to what's barely
there and maybe
not-quite yet
between the lines

to sit   taking
a stand and read
learning straightness
and when to bend
so we come
not to the End—

but once again
and again to And

A MAN LIVES IN A WORLD

A man lives in a world he builds for himself
from desires his flesh desires for itself
and from the views with which he eases for himself
fears with which he frightens himself
and from the love he loves himself with
and from the hate he hates himself with.

In summer he heads out past himself
and in the fall he returns to himself
and sees what he has done for himself
during the summer and what he hasn't done for himself
and takes account   and amounts to himself.

Natan Zach, Hebrew, 20th c.

ZAYIN : ז

Words are weapons
   of supplication—
forged in flames,
   like swords, they lick
or maim in naming's
   sheer adornment:
and who'd have thunk

it'd come to this,
   beneath the hiss
and buzz of fame,
   just the slow
hum of an angel's
   whatever-it-is
leading me in

to a day's interstices
   and modest claim
to what's there
   in the brightness,
like a light
   leaked from Eden—
it sustains . . .

EATING PARADISE

There is no recipe for this dish—
this meal of early evening stillness,
this light like a powder
                              over the harbor's
crushed lapis that lifts in its sinking
mixed with wisps of a silky distant
thought receding within that hour
the swifts reel
                    seeking meals
in high flies and crying out
through wheel and fall, then soaring
back for more—
                        there is no formula for this
twist in the spirit's little fit
and arousal we crave, calling, and then
recalling it: dusk, now,
along the quay,
                    though no more really know
than do those swifts (which may be swallows),
how this rendering finds and refines us
or where, in time, as time it goes.

FROM THE QUALMIST'S QUAIR

I.

Vapor clouding
from coiled shit,
hot air from
    mouths and lips—

face it, said the
dark's harpist—
is the everything
    everything is.

      ■

Sick of talk
we babble on,
one generation
    lapping another.

Earth remains
unchanged forever,
shrugs the skeptic.
    But does it?

      ■

Wisdom earned
learns vexation;

the more you know
   you know it hurts.

■

The fool (knows
all and) folds
his arms (closed)
   then eats (angry)

his (hungry) heart out . . .

■

Better a handful
of calm than
two of clutching
   at the wind . . .

two of grasping
for the wind . . .
two of chasing
   after wind . . .

II.
Look around:
Chance and Time
have at all
   again and again

and none know when
theirs will come
like schools of fish
    near nets stretched out

or birds at snares
fate has baited,
their days in flight
    (click) done.

    ■

Dead flies
rot and stink
up the finest
    oil and ointment

i.e., a
little stupidity
goes quite far
    when it comes

to spoiling what's
been bequeathed
from eternity,
    and one's honor.

And so I started
to hate my life,

my failings and failure
   under the sun

all that vapor
and clutching at wind,
and so I detested
   all that I'd done,

out with the air
   under the sun.

III.

I saw as well
a ruler's face
(like his palace)
   swell with corruption

and told myself
a god would judge
where evil existed,
   and what good was

though as we descend
to the issue of ends
the difference between
   beasts and men

grows hard to discern,
or so it seemed

through darkness dispersing
    thickened again

and then I thought
of those who were suffering:
Is *oppressed* a cardboard
    term to avoid

when they're everywhere
being deployed
and riven by forces
    deaf to their cries?

Don't be so surprised
at the poor man's neck
crushed by a knee
    come down from on high

and higher . . . Is
that just vapor
under the sun?
    His gasping for wind?

IV.

Thus the qualmist's
harping—Dark
days will still
    be many, and . . .

while the light
is sweet to the eyes
when all gets said
    what will survive

but vapor rising
from mouths and lips,
hot air
    from coiled shit?

So savor what
you see and drink,
and work itself—
    not what it brings.

In time, the castle's
masters will tremble—
the lines make it clear,
    its servants will stoop;

its mills depleted,
the grinding will stop,
and onlookers' views
    dim from within.

Its double doors
to the street will shut,

the bustle gradually
　　growing still

as the sound of a bird
gives you a start,
and song itself
　　dies away.

Walking uphill
becomes an ordeal;
every path is
　　lined with peril

as almond trees blossom
and the locust is bowed,
and capers budding
　　on bushes swell.

Everyone leaves
for the long dwelling,
as mourners gather
　　in the square—

before the silver
cord is snapped,
before the golden
　　bowl shatters

and the pitcher's broken
beside the spring,
and wheels to the cisterns'
   waters are crushed,

dust returns
to earth as it was,
breath to the place it
   blew through us from.

V.

All this I
thought I'd learned
and tried to teach,
   though wisdom remained

beyond my reach,
just beyond
and just as deep—
   and truly, who

could grasp it?

after Qohelet

CHET : ‎ח

I.

Chet is hard—not chard—
to say, like Van Gogh
or Bach, for some, it's
life itself in short,
i.e., it's strange
and likely strained at times
as such and so to speak
about it they say—*l'chayyim*.

II.

Or else, it points to the beast
within us who use it to bring
things that are hidden out
from behind what they had been
before, I thought, it's a lot
like a fence conjuring sides
as for a time we're alive
and then again we're not.

III.

An overly zealous few
insist it stands for the most

constituent stuff of existence—
or maybe just a disgust
or even disgrace and abasement
in knowing so very much
of life leaves us fearing
we're pitched on a cliff of mistakes.

LET'S NOT GET CARRIED AWAY

But let's not get carried away because
the translator shouldn't. We'll pass words on, calmly,
from one person to another, from one tongue to the lips
of others

without knowing that's what we're doing, like a father
passing his dead father's features
on to his son. He resembles neither.
He's just a mediator.

We'll remember what we had
in hand but let slip through,
what we own and what we don't—
and, we won't get carried away.
Cries and criers alike go under. Or, my lover
left some words behind, before she went her way,
so I might raise them for her.

And we'll no longer say to others
what was said to us. Silence is like a confession.
We shouldn't get carried away.

Yehuda Amichai, Hebrew, 20th c.

TET : ט

That *god* and *good*
   as English words
rub elbows,
   shoulders and—
though less likely—
   far more private
parts is something
   oddly absent
and at once

   a given in
the almost always
   resonant Scripture's
Hebrew since
   the deity there—
curiously plural
   in its inflection,
meaning more
   or less universal?—

saw what he'd done
   and said it was just
that: good

(*tov*), as when
one's *mazal* is
    (call it fortune),
for example,
    this persimmon
in its bowl—

    curve within
curve and amber
    flesh like a
melon's in
    an ocher skin
slightly bruised
    near mandarin
oranges set
    beside the window,

rain slanting
    past the pane,
a warplane roaring
    overhead
through December—
    Chinese masters,
and then Persian,
    often drew them,
which is to say,

drew them in
through it all,
    war and famine,
exile, shame—
    voids and ink stains—
clearly fine
    if less a given
than a gift
    made more vivid

strangely by
    the early morning
paper's *news*
    from a foreign
country come—
    so much it did
my heart inflame:
    Aleppo crushed,
the flight begun

    again and scores
of thousands hung
    not as though
between lives
    alone but over
nothing at all . . .

or maybe worse:
Please! Do not
   destroy!! There

are things here
   your children might
be able to use . . .
   What a great
victory . . . That
   used to be
a street, these
   were homes . . . this
is how it's happening

   now, . . . You see
a bomb falling
   from the sky,
you wait and close
   your eyes, waiting
to die, or realize
   you're still alive.
This is the feeling
   inside you, she said.

In Aleppo.
   Good god.

III

ON BEING
DRAWN

(for Terry Winters)

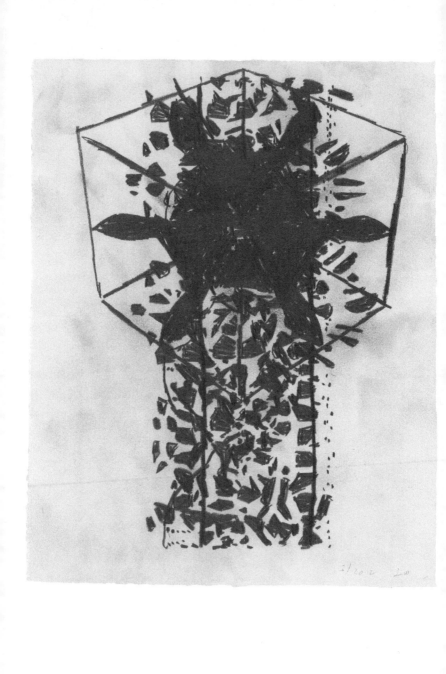

I

Drawing draws us in-
volving us further and stretches
attention it sketches reaching
inches in ink and grasps
graphite graphing drawing
draws us out of our cells
and selves extending thinking
into seeing what was
sensed or seen as something
once in hand an eye
or at the fingers' tips
it leads one on and into
depths and arcs as angles
curve through layered swerves
and lines as tines drawing
is first and quickest to
the quick and draw and yet it
slows and flows unfolds
in time raveling mine
it tries out signs along
a way a wavering it's a
doodle dancing within
its perfect incompletion

now a mesh and not a
mess a net at work
along a seam between us
drawing seems to hone
what might be true and turn
by turn it trains but doesn't
tame. Like runes. It tunes us.

II

Charcoal's quiet and chalky mist
seed a cone's emergence from its
sinking here now into the page
as   and of its absence and grays
there and not quite there yet mix.

■

This dark plant glows with its ground
and grows from a black fire of whiteness—
so boundlessness pulses, nearly in hand.
Its smudged halo holds, like a kiss,
creation's lipstick, a fooling around.

■

The nerve and zinc ascent of it:
descending extension in every direction—
knots of cinder and brightness as one
wash of ash through which it hums
beneath the skin   these paths are thought.

III

Odd how globs form morulae
or constellations of single cells
evolve as clocks of grape-like clouds
and scarlet clusters hovering near
smears of a maculate whiteness become
the drifting stalk and jot of an *i* . . .

■

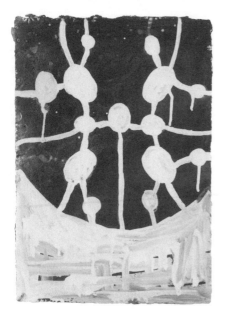

Neurons fire
in black and white
(gouache and graphite)
and unlike angels
don't expire
with ignition
along a spine
reaching the head
we wander into
the frame and opening
of an interim
installation
to which all roads
have suddenly led

■

The eye slides beyond the rendering's
frame and out through just about
everything now we're seeing there
in these blinding lines, elided . . .

■

Rhyme's a rhizome,
rhyme is loam.
When it's foam
the poem's not done.
The poem's not done
until it's a dome
(the dome itself
is a kind of poem)
and even then
there's more to come,
as the rhizome roams
and its phonemes run
up and slantwise
down at once,
through its phloem—
the poem is one.
Through its phloem.
The poem is done.

IV

There is a score to all
that isn't said a constant
buzz or hum enlarged
a pulse that soon becomes
like something sung or spoken
within there is a string
no, there are wavering

violins we bring
a tension like a wish
a wind along a wall
or laundry line and clothespins
marking time with keys
shifting through an un-
quaint calm and now
a chaos of tangled thinking's
twine, in a drawer,
a silent roar the world
is bound by secret knots,
they say, though what that means
is hard to know and flickers
so, also, and really
are those knots a noose
that hangs or ties that bind
our being stuck or held
together like a bridge
to build and cross or maybe
draw on or up
so no one can there is
a score to all that . . .

V

Ink can twist it-
self around
and form a spring
from which things come
to figure infinity
in a glyph
or couple facing a pale
gray distance within
one
    another's ominous
shades further off and frailer
still but in the picture just
as well—like a trick
or quip—LIFE it seems
is penciled in a
biblically cryptic script

VI

This writing's on and off the wall
and tells us what it is and why
we're so   intent on understanding
a layered saying that seems to say it
all and nothing in particular
just like everything seen by those
who know it shows at best the whole
in part that grows with the telling
and spell   dangling   in between
like   someone listening into a
certain sort of uncertainty speaking
of uncertainty as a song
of songs tangled truly in our
being led along a luminous
line singed and fringe within
the singing's seeing seeing us through

VII

An ark so dark it
glows with its holding
the nothing it knows
within its unfolding

composes now
a hardening spark's
unhidden power
unbidden black

in diamond white
as softening graphite
crystal flaking
gently breaks

into an opaque
night of florescence
over a field
behind a fence

where a king's thinking
of slipping tenses
and the ancient art
of riding wakes

(or maybe only
a day's mistakes)
here at the pointed
end of a pencil

from a parcel
and that's a start
as ink shines
in the king's heart

2009

Lw 2011

VIII

This world's dotty matrix calls
    and draws us toward a broken cause's
lozenged rose or window-wall
    and whorl or just a kind of clausal
contract-with-the-viewer you
    might be paying attention now
to the verb itself as somehow
    pay implies a currency in
a thicker economy of concentration
    and price that rhymes with sacrifice
which may be why these vortices bear
    spheres and diamonds in their whir
this morning's something we almost feel
    or feel but can't quite put into words
or give a name to   and that's the pearl
    or cone of dark that lets light through
a future via repetition's
    asking once and then again
a tension's moving around within
    what might be only a fancy screen
savored and caught in a nick of Time
    on a page we drift across
the day and toward its deckled edge

giving way to what it suggests—
beauty's keeping secrets between us
    or screaming in silence to be seen
making a music of its emergency
    sail to a small magnificence or
this eddy's swirl's a pendant to
    a listening that's an end and means:
an eerie earring funneling care
    as hours that are always theres.

IX

How *does* this drawer hold it
    all within a space
along a trace left
    on a surface marked
as such the world is drawn
    with water from a well
and then a gun or wagon,
    now a loan against
collateral, or interest on
    a bank account and maybe
a conclusion? Drapes
    are drawn so light gets in
or doesn't; someone draws
    attention drawing even
in a race he's drawn to,
    drawn aside or else
asunder, thus the luck
    of the draw we call it
has the drawing card
    drawing cheers, or blood,
a breath or blank or cello's
    bow, and so he drew
a bath or on a pipe

as she drew fire and ducked
the goose was shot and plucked
    then drawn as dawn drew near
they drew together playing
    on to a draw drawing
back and again to the
    drawing board and plans
to hatch, or hatches to sketch
    like poems, yes, always
more to draw on there with-
    in the proverbial drawer.

IV

YOD : י

In this tradition
smallness stands
tall through all
lending a hand
to creation

And so a squiggle
crowns our scrawl
as eminence bends
down to call
us through duration

HEARSING

He was on his way in the dream
across a sea of sorts to Hearsing,
he remembered, knowing the place
didn't exist as such but rose
up within him nonetheless
almost magically like a meniscus
over something he'd have heard
during the day after they
began rehearsing all those parts
that they'd play as each of their lives
more or less and in the end
was improvised very plausibly
though possibly too he was simply
hearing things once again
long before he'd come near them
simple things slipping through him
much like sleep or blood and breathing
in the way it all played out
in his dream of sailing to Hearsing.

KAF : כ

Sometimes a palm's a lamp
    whose tilt alters a plan
long held-to— or a plea
through which we'd suddenly leap

LÁMED : ל

Its leg buckling as it extends
up toward something always beyond it,
it's lamed, and maybe sublime. Wounded
loving learning, its goal a goad,
this letter holds   for learning love.

HOW COULD IT HAPPEN

Who'd have known this sadness would turn
　　on a dime into a
　　　　　　　　　　kind of madness,
　　　　making my mind a hell as rivers
of fire ran through my eyes and swept
　　　　　　away what it was I'd
　　long been,
　　　　　　　　　tossing it like
a boat across
　　　　　　　a sea of pulsing
　　　blood as waves
　　　　　ripped apart
　　its planks and ribs
loosened as salty ocean rushed in—

when, for wanting, I was taken
into a suddenly
　　　　　　　arid dimension
　　　of depth like a desert
split wide open
to swallow a pride in its insistence.
　　　　How could I have

known it would happen?
How could it happen
   that I've known?

AS:

The river's parting into four
rivers running through the world
to the ends or end of the world
the light of beginning beginning to end

the light of beginning which hasn't yet been
in rivers of letters running through words
needing Eden's injured green
angeled garden, Eden's song

MEM : מ

Thinking's chariot starts with it:
this angels' tank of measured listening,
wherein mum's the ready word
riding *mem*, the mouth closed,
lips resting along one another,
kissing silence and yielding *hmmm*.
  Wheels of scorn and praise
  turn and bear its throne.

NUN : נ

It stands for almost nothing—
this kitelike flame of soul-hovering
yellow and blue somehow fluttering
over a string and in
a wind that's always blowing
face it   again and again
amazing with a quiet glowing
so thin and yet it
fills the room and burns
through skin   like almost nothing

CAN YOU HEAR ME?

Can you hear me?
There at the back,
yes? Testing
1, 2, 3 . . . ?

This is working?
Great. Everything's
working? Great.
Just checking—

you never know
what exactly's
getting through,
do you?   It's

a little like the
day, years ago,
I was on
a radio show—

Sound Check,
that was its name,
though at the time
I didn't know

what it was called,
so, when
I was sent
into the studio

and the host looked
up and said—
"Just follow my lead . . .
This is Sound Check . . ."

I kept staring
slightly terrified
into his eyes
trying to hear

if we were live
or only rehearsing,
which is, in its way,
always the question.

SAMEKH : ס

Even the thought of roundness raises
hopes of arriving into a middle
and being between where everything happens
and can because it hasn't yet—
the hole of it filled entirely
with nothing but a faint possibility
lying there in a line drawn
round in the mind like mountains
encircling a town   full of sound
and when you're near   its fountains

AYIN : עַ

Now he takes it into his mouth—
this hinged morsel and fork to infinity.
Now it takes him into its truth—
this glyph giving us eye and spring,

source and portal to just about everything
deep within him, and once like Jerusalem,
or maybe the brightness of every beginning
glimmering there in the letters and teaching

whose facets refract and reflect without end
the absolute in us, which always depends.

I WENT OUT TOWARD MY LIFE

I went out toward my life, my will set strong—and raised
                                          to the power
of seventy tongues. The gates were guarded, it seemed,
                                          by translators
moving among them. They helped me. But now they're
                                          gone,
    and my heart returns, alone, to its first home.

Yehuda Amichai, Hebrew, 20th c.

This   voice   this   mouth   this   hole   this   snail
This   choice   this   month   this   quarrel   this   pearl
This   sylph   this   moth   this   chill   this   fool
This   self   this   host   this   lull   this   hill
This   smell   this   mist   this   mill   this   pool
This   balm   this   kiss   this   boil   this   ghoul
This   lamb   this   hiss   this   boss   this   pull
This   sham   this   thrush   this   poise   this   pall
This   mess   this   curse   this   gauze   this   gall
This   guess   this   cost   this   muzzle   this   hall

V

THESE PIECES

adjust the air
or its
pressure the space around them where
lines meet

sometimes and
sometimes not who knows how or
why, really
it's happening here, just so
through this poem
of a room we roam
inside ourselves, these stanzas

▪

Is it beauty

buoyed

up or

ungainli-
ness itself as such
that holds us here

&

what's

holding this one

                    there
              above us?

        Hmmm—

        not clear at all but clearly
        something
                        beyond
              itself

   ■

              Neither right
        nor wrong, not even
        left
                exactly
           out   or—

        just the thrall and
              soaring fall

        and call of

   ■

        Are these
        songs of degrees
                    increments

in their way
of an inter-
rupted descent

or broken descant

strung from fishing
line or guy-
wired (like words) hovering
in a breeze within that
plays these beams
and cords like chords

■

O

Yes—

Oh

No,
not this
shadow
longer than the
joy which is
just that—

                                    Yes

                    Joy

                              and

              another collap-

        sing into a

                    crouch to hold

    on or leap

          up to shout with more

    of that

                same uneasy ec-

                          static (moving, why?)

    delight—

                    Uh-oh,

              no   not

        that   Yes

              that

                    No/Yes

                                to seeing limbed

          bronze beneath those sky

                        blues is why

    ■

Sly,
a little
    wily, and why
        not

who's to say it
isn't sublime
or
    just that something
more we're always
    falling into or for
and possibly from   having
failed
        to reach
it or for it

        slipping

    into space
weighted with waiting
        almost defying
gravity's say in the whole

matter
of its unfolding

recomposing
at once itself
and, yes, you
too, viewer, reader, hanger-
on to what's
been hung are
installed within this
installation site-
specifically
and oh so perfectly
pitched in
its ambivalence

■

Go figure, the figures seem to
say—in their almost
swaying

how it is
that what we mean
is what we stand
between,

always
an after and then
what

was before that always
at least

two things come
together (or more)
to form—

"all that abstraction, it's
so human."

for Joel Shapiro

TSADI : צ

Someone is walking by a roadside head bowed low
eyes it seems to the ground although in fact
he's looking within and gone as it were fishing
in those murky waters for   what exactly is it
not in silence per se as thinking is a
sort of talking to one's self or ghosts whatever
either is or isn't really ears begin to stir
not yet a sound that spells more a humming
through a grayness call it a patience maybe saintly
or indulgence just so long as its longing's sung

QUF : ק

Fucked art thou, with luck, o reader within the palace
    within the palette within the disquiet within, who tilts his
    letters into the light of the mind's muttering unto itself,
    releasing their sounds to the *whirlpool fierce* of an ear *to*
    draw creations in—

Who brings forth a kiss of circumference, the scripts
    hooked and loosened and linking, through moths of
    minutes and months like wind, out of a god whose name
    is Gone . . .

Fukkit and lukky art thou in the wind moving marjoram
    into the mint, the fuzz and down of one grazing the
    raised ribs of the other, the essences borne—

Pheromones suddenly wafting, your eye catching the
    gradient greens and veinlike patterns, the gray stubble of
    sage's tongue, thick oregano's glister and whorl, stalks of
    thyme spiking the air on a kitchen porch or distant slope,
    its lavender flower lit in June;

The blue film of night's end rolling into white near dawn,
    the light by which you know a friend, the ancients
    explain, from six feet off—or a wolf from a dog;

The pulse of morning bougainvillea, its papery bracts in a
    breeze like prayer, its bezeled ruby beginnings morphing
    into pinks- and magentas-to-come, cream-tipped corollas
    on perfect display, style and stigma sheathing the anther;

And then—creeping Christians' dusky luster, in the shade
at noon;
Almonds swelling jade drupes into the sinking summer;
Pomegranate's garnet, pendant, containing—against the
green of its arch and stretch—six hundred seeds dark
with light, glinting through the cracks in its skin;
Fucked, art thou, and lucky, who translates it into the day
as blessed—
So blessed as in blasted in a way art thou, in whom this
knowing is strengthened in bringing you down to sinews
of creaking knees, wrestling the gust of a given moment's
giving, like vapor, and strangely grateful;

Blessèd art thou whose petitions are curses, whose fuck
touches an innermost chamber, waking the letters from
their slumber;
Blessèd the consonants funneling vowels, in scripture's
offering;
Blessèd the spirit's unfurling within a word set or typed or
scrawled, as not quite deciphered codes of soul;
Blessèd even the stink and politic rot of the day's
pronouncements on high, *Liver of the blaspheming Jew, gall
of goat, and slips of yew*,
And, in action as Evil: the concrete Lego-like bunker and
tower, bunker and tower, barbwired cabbage and vines,
shadows gliding as crows fly across the road to the holy

of hills and prefab shacks, from which herd-like thugs
    emerge, watching and then descending through a slope-
    stepping prance, fringes trailing—their dance sick with
    a stiffened faith, wicking and blotching their map of
    state, like a cancered scan, eating away at its language
    and letters, as *One* yields *gun* or *none* or *bone* . . . where
    lips meet and part in the *b* of all that's brutal and also
    insidious, in the possibly pointless battle—
Evoking the hundred blessings the rabbis say need to be
    uttered daily, reading the number—*me'ah* (hundred)—
    into the word for *what*, or *mah*: "*What* does Becoming
    your God ask of you?" (Deuteronomy 10:12);
And blessèd is never quite knowing, exactly, what those
    blessings should be.

THE GHAZAL OF WHAT'S MORE THAN REAL

for David Shulman

And now words reach us as Persian meets Urdu,
making ours real, and then some, like David's do

in an English he's always leaving behind
and returning to, as it happens, like dew

on grass or a vine's blue grapes—even a glass
left out in a garden his poets imbue

with powers. Still, he'd be the first to tell you—
it's a mirage. Meaning's mortgage. Maybe true.

True and not true. Glistening, as we see it—
a kind of beloved. Something desire drew,

drawing us too. . . . Again lines are leading him
beyond himself, and soon he's bidding adieu

to ease, with ease, in every way. It pleases
him, who'll share his secrets, as though they were new,

so they will be. So leaning and learning meet
along a mind's mirror, coupling there, a clue.

Residue . . . of a slow knowing—as fog stops
the brown mountain: *I imagine, therefore you*

are. Therefore, imagine, so that I might be
with you, wandering friend, when these debts come due.

REISH : ר

again for (and from) Terry Winters

Beginning being an engine's emergence
late in a game an *O* an opening how and again really
already a budding or not knotted here we've come from
                                                    behind
behold ahead of what we've done or are we
hosting hosted something haunted coping copied (closer)
                                                    coded
keeping to a line of slipping feeling for a formal coming
                                        always into being a
gin again within that fate in the game as flesh (mapped)
                                        we're caught (cut)
in thought's reaching into the grain
of things the ground a pining rippling a rubbing of rings
                                                    widens
a dark divides us from and into selves as cells
shifting not quite black to white but back from tight through
                                            seeds of seeing
a start like spores released or doors at once beyond and still
                                        at heart a turning
up as one the embers' umber floats a ball which holds it all
the lightness of its lifting so

she's seen within what's felt without the frame maintains its
distance bringing digits near a surface bearing what we hear
and now at hand inflected there is that an ear or crown we
wear the swarms of voicings scanned connect the
dots through doubt or debt
and wing it

SHIN : ש

1

Sure you know. Know you don't. Listen. I am listening. He's listening. Not listening. Listing. Sure he is. Ssshhh . . . Or, give it a listen.

2

At which I ceas't, and listen'd them a while. Listinythe a while and ye shall see: Sor Juana says I'm not. While they listened for the distant hunt. The sick man would listen for her coming. Listening in to the news of the world: the fun that was going on in the kitchen.

3

And there we were—reading and wearing all this weaving. Men of letters. Ladies of our alphabets. For a spell. Licking and taking a licking. As we liked. Killed. Lied. Leaned. Remained. Linked in our maiming. Of heirs. Renowned. A rippling. Every cercle causing other wyder than hymselve was. From, and toward, the shattered names.

4

Into the house of sound. Unbounding . . .

5

This is a hearing and that's a tree-ring. One is nearing what
was far, which brought you here, into a clearing, and these
are years, that much is sheer (cheers), a peace of something
always missing, surpassing understanding . . .

6

Understood . . . from that fissure song ascends . . . Draw me
after. After the beards will lead us there, into the bared trans-
lation. A being dared. That black-and-bluish ink (we're
bleeding) disturbs so—so we swerve. Beware, you are—
and aren't—what you were. Now herkneth every maner
man that English understonde can.

7

Under the Scorpions tayle—standeth the Altar. His head
came in contact with a sort of step, of which there are sev-
eral projecting from the sides of a dock, and are . . . techni-
cally called Altars. The incense altar she heard was inward.
Why is it called a site of slaughter—

8

among the letters, called . . . into a smallness, overcoming.
A harshness. Or harness. Shhhh. An easy greenness by the
graves. Engraved. Listen. Winter windflower. Silvery sky.

WHAT THE BEARD SAID, III

is, just now, beyond me
softly—as a kind of mercy?—
here within the fat
book's saying that
to ascend's in fact
to sink into the heart of
what's on high beginning
with what's right in front
of our eyes and ears above
all else or else beneath
them when they're close
to being closed to dying
to the world we go
now now it isn't so
hard to imagine something
coming from nothing and not
for nothing as they say it
might just be your lucky day
or maybe someone else's nothing
come to something or
something to naught is what I
thought I heard there in what the
beard (softly) seemed to be saying

TAV : ת

for RS, targuman supreme

After an awe an anthill an ache   an anvil already an
altar's ambition   admission   an almond and amber
audition   an almost always arriving antiphonal
alchemical   ash   an asking   asking again

                                        Between—
bother brother breath brothel   battle blather but
Bible *Bildung*   bad bard   bride   bridle

                              Carry cabal
cavil cannibal   chariots calling channels culling   civil
chisel centrifugal   chronically creeping   conceit
cleaves   choral corporal conjure chore   cherubs cover
cagey chords   canticles conquer cant   cowardice
craving can   cures   cynosure   censure   constraints
condole   corrupt   come-hither

                              Danger—daimons
dangling darkly daunting dictate dazzling dare: *decide decide
decide decide*   deceive defy   delight derive

                                    Earning
Eden's echoes   errant ethos   ego's Egypt   envoy
envy exhorting

          Follow filigree find fool's

                                    Gold Gould
ghouls goads ghosts guise *Geist* gist guess guests

                                    His hers
hearse hearth   hoaxes host humbled hired heralds

                                         Ink
insists—infecting

          Joints joust jaded jokers   jinn joy
justice

     Kiblah kabuki kabbalah   kamikaze keister ken
kenosis   kinesis   kiddush kin   kibitz keyhole kink

                                         Like
lachrymose labyrinth labor ladder lattice let's   lacunae
legacy larceny larval libel   liable limp laurel   limpid
lip-synch logos lokum   loan loin loom   lambent liminal
layers lie   Lucifer's lyre   lumen-lust

My my

mime   make-light-of   make-much-of make-use-of
make-off-with make-out-with make-over make-up
make-time make-tracks   make-way make-waves
make-do   me-too   medium middleman mess
messianic   mishegas mensch   metonym morph much-as

Nerve   nag   nigh . . .

Oh obliquity   only own

Partially
plausibly   prove provide   puzzle prism pleasures pluck

Quoth   quark   queasy quotient quest

Rumor ruins
rub rubble rooms   render rattle rent   relish
relinquish replenish   relay rely reframe refrain   refract
redux   reduce redress   radiant ragpicker

Sacrum
sanctum   savor sadness savvy   sympathy   scholia
scruple schizoid scheme   screen scream   seemly séance
secret shadow seizure segue   shelf-life sequel   shoptalk

shouldn't   schnorrer should   slug shrug   signals
singly sing sigh   so   so-called   sort-of   spells
spooky story

             Telos tel telepathy   Te-Deum   tedium
toad to-do   today tentacles tomorrow temerity
tentative tenancy   tensility tents   techne texture tact
tactic trick tactility   tangents tilt   time's tang   tow
toil toll torque torts torture traitor trait target *targum*
trance transcend   treasure-trap trickle-down trompe-
l'oeil Trojan-Horse   trot troth truth tribute   trans-
trust thresholds tryst   troubadour trouble   trying
tribunal   twin tinge twined tune

                         Underrated understated
underwritten understood

Volatile valor votive vapors   viral vows   volley valley
voice   veiled void   various valences vectors verge
virgin vertigo   verse vessel vestibule   vestige vouch
virtual vulnerable vulture   vintage violent visit

                              While
watch-it   weird wagers   warily   wild willed wound
wreathes wraiths   weddings writhing writing whence

X

Yikes yips yoke   yeah yeah   yaw yank yon yearn   yield
you   yours—

Zeugmatically,

CODA:

Into the end-
lessness of our alpha-
    bets through a being
        alive-or-dead
    to all that might
be said of our seeing
or where we've been
    diminished or made
        to feel like kings
or queens of creation's
brim hearing

clearly a fading
echo of what's
    beyond us but also
        near, and even
    welling as never
before   and again
within these letters
    (from the garden
        now . . . a wren)
I'd known all along
as if in a dream.

A NOTE ABOUT THE AUTHOR

Peter Cole was born in Paterson, New Jersey, in 1957. The author of five previous books of poems, he has also translated widely from Hebrew and Arabic—medieval and modern. He is the recipient of many honors, including a Guggenheim Fellowship, an American Academy of Arts and Letters Award in Literature, a PEN Translation Prize for Poetry, a National Jewish Book Award, and a MacArthur Fellowship. He divides his time between Jerusalem and New Haven.